Craft Lacing

Mania

D1529735

Craft Lacing
Mania

Anouchka Galvani

David and Charles

A DAVID & CHARLES BOOK
This edition copyright © David & Charles Limited 2005

David & Charles is an F+W Publications Inc. company
4700 East Galbraith Road
Cincinnati, OH 45236

First published in the US in 2005
Reprinted 2007
First published in the UK in 2005 as *Scoubidou Mania*

First published in France as *Scoubidou Mania* in 1998
Text and illustrations copyright © Fleurus 1998

Anouchka Galvani has asserted her right to be identified as author of this
work in accordance with the Copyright, Designs and Patents Act, 1988.

A catalogue record for this book is available from the British Library.

ISBN 0 7153 2479 9 paperback (US only)

Printed in China by SNP Leefung
for David & Charles
Brunel House   Newton Abbot   Devon

The author and publisher have made every effort to ensure that all the
instructions in this book are accurate and safe, and therefore cannot accept
liability for any resulting injury, damage or loss to persons or property
however it may arise.

Visit our website at www.davidandcharles.co.uk

David & Charles books are available from all good bookshops; alternatively
you can contact our Orderline on 0870 9908222 or write to us at FREEPOST
EX2 110, D&C Direct, Newton Abbot, TQ12 4ZZ (no stamp required UK
only); US customers call 800-289-0963 and Canadian customers call
800-840-5220.

Enter the wacky world of craft lacing with these crazy and colorful projects!

Craft lacing (also known as Boondoggle and Scoubidou) is a fast and fun way to create funky forms. By bending, weaving, knotting and making all kinds of special moves with the craft-lacing threads (also known as scoubidou threads), you can transform them into dozens of weird and wonderful shapes. You can buy the threads in many toy and craft stores.

Follow the basic techniques shown, and become an expert in no time! Then move on to the brilliant projects to create over 30 animals and accessories to keep yourself or to give away as great gifts.

Contents

6   **The basics**
7   **Classic techniques**

The projects

14 Mini-people

18 Pen pals

20 Animal magic

24 Cool keyrings

28 Juicy jewellery

30 Accessorize now!

34 Pocahontas family

36 Numbers and letters

40 Playground fun

The basics

Scoubidou threads

There are three different types of scoubidou thread: hollow, solid and flat. You can use any type of scoubidou thread to make up the projects in this book. However, if you want to reinforce your scoubidou thread you should use hollow strands, which you can strengthen by inserting lengths of wire.

Starting off your scoubidou

Standard knot

Take 2 scoubidou threads. Cut each one into two 45cm (18in) lengths. Tie the 4 strands together.

Standard knot with double loop

Take 2 scoubidou threads and halve them. Tie a knot to make a double loop.

Basic tool kit

- scissors
- glue
- wire and wire-cutters

Be careful!

You should always use wire-cutters under the supervision of an adult.

Hidden knot

Take 2 scoubidou threads. Make a cross at their centres. Knot one thread around the other. Plait your scoubidou and your starting knot will stay hidden.

1-thread loop

Take 2 scoubidou threads. Find the middle of the first (blue) thread and halve it. Pass your green thread behind your blue thread. Knot the green thread at its centre around the blue thread to make a blue loop.

Classic techniques

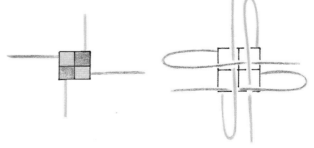

Finishing off your scoubidou

Apply a little fast-drying glue to your last row. Leave to dry thoroughly and trim your threads.

Reinforcing your scoubidou work

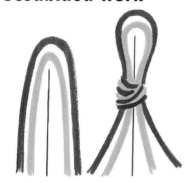

As you tie your starting knot, slide a length of wire into it and pull tight. Plait your scoubidou around this length of wire.

Reinforcing your thread

You must use hollow thread for this. Insert a length of wire into your thread, leaving excess wire at both ends.

Square scoubidou

1 Halve one pink thread and one mauve thread both 90cm (36in) in length. Tie a standard knot with a double loop.

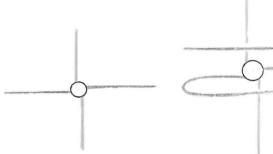

2 If you want your sides to be in alternate colours, lay threads in the same colour opposite each other. Start your scoubidou.

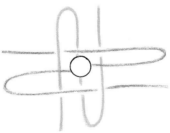

3 Plait the first row and pull it tight.

4 Plait your second row. Pull your threads tight and repeat this process until you reach your desired length.

Round scoubidou

1 Take 2 x 90cm (36in) threads, one green and one blue. Make a 1-thread loop by knotting the green thread over the blue loop.

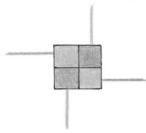

2 Plait your first row in the same way as for the square scoubidou. Pull tight.

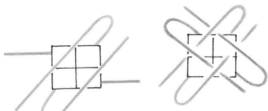

3 Lay 2 ends diagonally, as shown in the diagram. Plait and tighten.

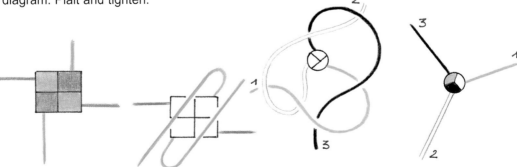

4 Turn your work around and reposition your threads as at the end of step 2. Repeat this process until you reach your desired length.

3-strand scoubidou

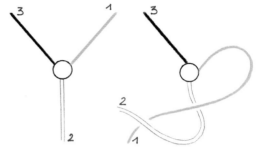

1 Tie a standard knot with 3 x 45cm (18in) threads. Separate the threads out and arrange them as shown in the diagram. Cross thread 1 over thread 2 and let go.

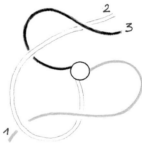

2 Cross thread 2 over thread 3 and let go.

3 Pass thread 3 through the loop in thread 1. Tighten well. Reposition your threads as per step 1. Continue in this way until you reach your desired length.

Rectangular scoubidou (8 strands)

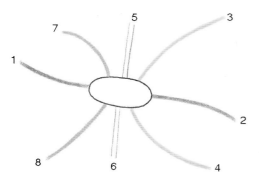

1 Take 1 x 90cm (36in) thread in blue and 3 x 60cm (24in) threads (1 yellow, 1 pink, 1 white). Knot the threads at their centre using yellow thread and lay them out as shown.

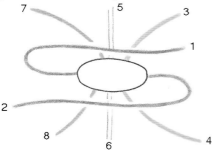

2 Pass thread 1 over the knot to make a loop. Pass thread 2 over the knot to make a loop.

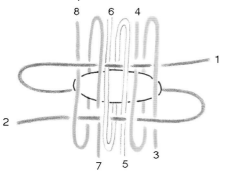

3 Plait threads 3, 4, 5, 6, 7 and 8 as shown in the diagram.

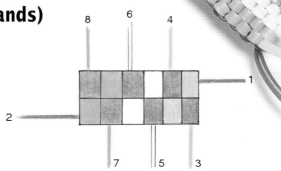

4 Tighten to form a rectangle made up of 12 small coloured squares.

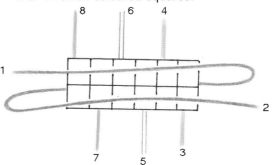

5 Start your second row by laying out the threads as shown in the diagram.

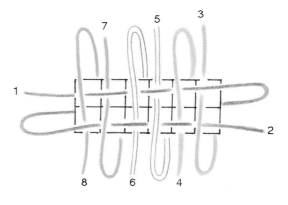

6 Plait your scoubidou. Your threads will end up in the position you started from (step 1). Repeat until you reach your desired length.

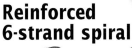

6-strand round scoubidou

Reinforced 6-strand spiral

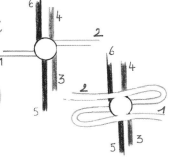

1 Take 6 x 45cm (18in) threads: 1 green, 1 pink, 1 white, 1 black, 1 blue and 1 yellow. Tie a standard knot and arrange your threads as shown.

2 Thread your yellow thread over your green thread and let go.

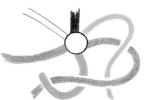

3 Thread the green thread over the pink thread and let go.

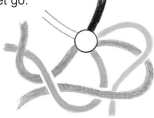

4 Thread the pink thread over the blue thread and let go.

5 Thread the blue thread over the white thread and let go.

6 Thread the white thread over the black thread and let go.

7 Thread the black thread into the loop of the yellow thread and pull tight. Reposition the threads as in step 1 and repeat.

1 Take 1 x 90cm (36in) scoubidou thread in white, 1 x 45cm (18in) in purple and 1 x 45cm (18in) in black. Thread the 3 strands through your keyring clasp, keeping your white thread on top. Ensure that the lengths hanging down on either side of the clasp are even. When your threads are even, secure them to the clasp with a 2cm (¾in) length of wire cut with wire-cutters. Tighten well.

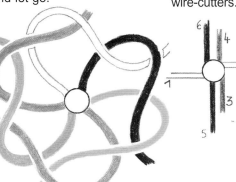

2 **First row** Separate your threads out and arrange them as shown. Pass thread 1 over the knot towards the right and thread 2 over the knot to the left.

3 Weave threads 3, 4, 5 and 6. Tighten well to make a rectangle made up of 8 small squares.

4 **Second row** Divide your work up into two squares each containing 4 small squares. Arrange your threads as shown in the diagram. Using the second diagram as a guide, pass thread 1 above the diagonal of the rectangle. Pass thread 2 below the diagonal in the opposite direction.

5 Weave your threads in groups across the diagonals of the 2 squares. Tighten the threads before starting your next row.

6 **Third row** Place thread 1 below the diagonal of the rectangle. Place thread 2 above the diagonal of the rectangle in the opposite direction. Weave the threads over the diagonals of the two small squares.

7 Tighten well. Your threads will be back to their starting position. Repeat until you reach your desired length. Apply a little glue to your final row.

8 You could reinforce your scoubidou using 1, 2 or 3 lengths of wire.

11

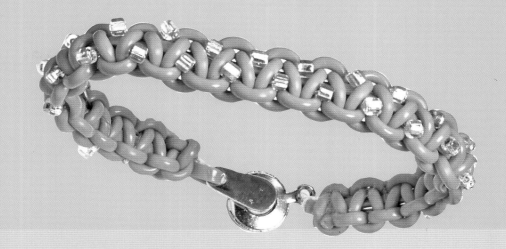

The
Projects

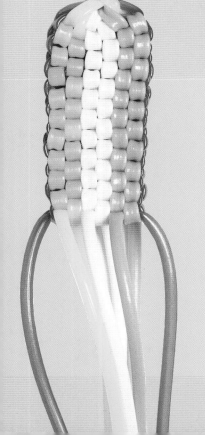

Mini-people

You will need...

- 1 x 90cm (36in) hollow scoubidou thread in green
- glue
- 1 ping-pong ball painted green
- nylon thread (20cm/8in)
- scissors and wire-cutters
- 1 x 8cm (3¼in) and 1 x 9cm (3½in) length of wire
- large clear glass beads 9mm (⅜in) in diameter in red (x 2) and dark green (x 2)
- medium-sized clear glass beads 5mm (³⁄₁₆in) in diameter in red (x 9), pale green (x 8), dark green (x 3) and yellow (x 12)
- 1 x 9cm (3½in) pipe-cleaner in dark green (arms)
- 1 x 12cm (4¾in) pipe-cleaner in dark green (legs)

Green guy

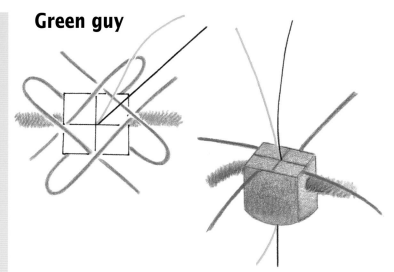

1 Cut your green scoubidou thread into two 45cm (18in) lengths. Start from the base of the body. Start off a reinforced round scoubidou with an added nylon thread. Thread the legs into a row 5mm (³⁄₁₆in) from your starting point. Plait your scoubidou over 6cm (2⅜in).

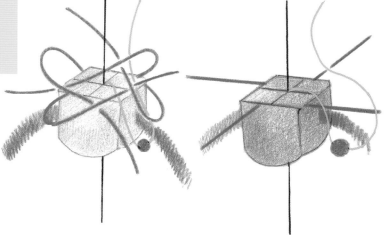

2 Thread the first of your medium-sized red beads onto your nylon thread 1.5cm (⅝in) from the start as shown in the diagram. Place the nylon thread back into the centre, leaving the bead to hang free. Finish your row and tighten. Pull on the nylon thread so your bead hangs at the side. Place the remaining 8 beads around the body over approx. 3cm (1⅛in).

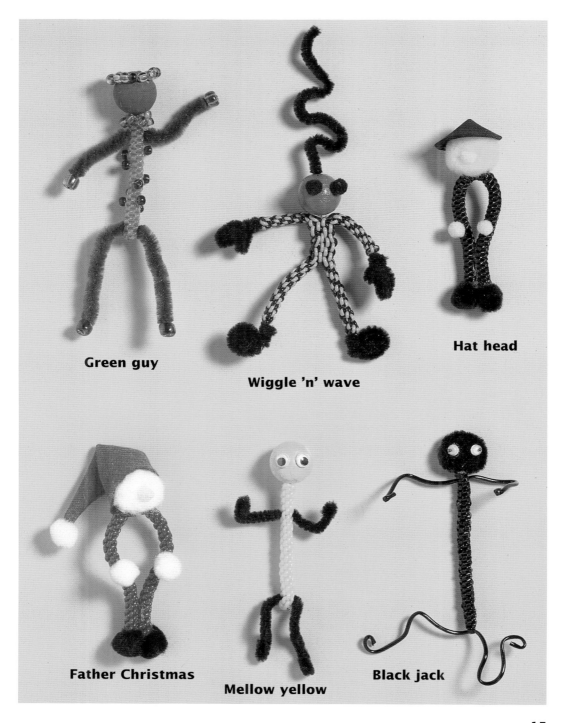

Green guy

Wiggle 'n' wave

Hat head

Father Christmas

Mellow yellow

Black jack

15

Mini-people

Wiggle 'n' wave

You will need...
- 2 x 90cm (36in) scoubidou threads in sky blue
- 2 x 90cm (36in) scoubidou threads in black
- 3 black pipe-cleaners
- 2 small pompoms 7mm (¼in) in diameter
- 1 ping-pong ball painted blue
- 2 x 10cm (4in) lengths of wire (for reinforcing)
- scissors and wire-cutters
- glue

3 Thread on the arms 5.5cm (2⅛in) from your starting point in the same way as for the legs. Weave until you have a 6cm (2⅜in) long scoubidou. Apply a little glue to your final row and trim your scoubidou threads.

Glue the head onto the remaining wire and secure. Make a necklace from your 8 green beads and some nylon. Tie the ends together and glue on under the head.

Cut a 9cm (3½in) length of wire. Using the diagram as a guide, thread on your beads. Tie the ends of the crown together and glue onto the head. Glue one large red glass bead onto the ends of each of the legs, and the large glass beads onto the arms.

Mellow yellow

Make the yellow stick man using the same method as for green guy. Use a 6cm (2⅜in) round scoubidou for the body; add moving eyes.

Black jack

Make a 7.5cm (3in) long round scoubidou. Start from a hidden knot. Thread a reinforced scoubidou thread 15.5cm (6⅛in) in length under the knot to make the legs and tighten well. Thread an 11cm (4⅜in) reinforced scoubidou thread into a row 7cm (2¾in) from your starting point to make the arms. To make the head, wind an 8cm (3⅛in) pipe-cleaner around itself and glue it together. Glue on 5mm (³⁄₁₆in) moving eyes, then glue the head onto the body. Hold it in place while it dries.

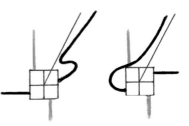

1 Start by making a hidden knot and plait a reinforced round scoubidou in blue and black. Leave 5mm (³⁄₁₆in) excess wire at the start of your scoubidou. Weave your scoubidou over 4cm (1½in) to make a leg. Leave that section. Make up the other leg in the same way. Bring your work together to make the chest. To make this section, keep the 2 black threads in the centre with your wire. Do not include these threads when weaving the scoubidou for the chest.

2 Bring the two legs together and weave a rectangular 6-strand scoubidou. Plait the trunk over 2.5cm (1in).

3 To make the two scoubidous for the arms, start to work a round scoubidou. Reinforce each scoubidou. Weave for 3cm (1¹⁄₈in). Finish off with a little glue. Leave 5mm (³⁄₁₆in) excess wire sticking out.

4 Glue pompoms onto the head, and the head onto the body. Make a hole in the head and glue on 13cm (5in) of pipe-cleaner for hair. Cut a 9cm (3¹⁄₂in) length of pipe-cleaner for the hands and 7.5cm (3in) for the feet. Wind the pipe-cleaner tightly around itself, then glue round the wire.

Father Christmas

You will need...
- 2 x 90cm (36in) scoubidou threads in red
- 1 small pink pompom (7mm/¹⁄₄in)
- 15mm (⁵⁄₈in) pompoms in black (x 2) and white (x 3)
- 1 white pompom 25mm (1in) in diameter
- red felt
- nylon thread
- scissors and glue

1 Start off your round scoubidou with a hidden knot. Weave for 14.5cm (5³⁄₄in). Finish off with a little glue and leave to dry. Trim your threads. Apply glue to a 1.5cm (⁵⁄₈in) area at each end of your scoubidou. Bring the two ends together and stick them to each other. Secure the ends by tying a length of nylon thread around your scoubidou. Pull tight. Leave overnight, then remove the nylon thread.

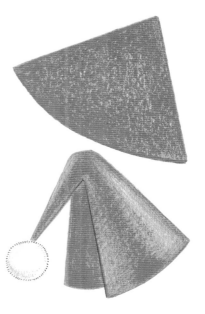

2 Cut out an equilateral triangle with 9cm (3¹⁄₂in) sides to make the hat. Fold and glue it onto the large white pompom at a slant. Glue your 3 white pompoms onto the hands and hat, glue on the black pompoms to make boots and the pink pompom to make a nose. Glue the head onto the body.

Hat head
You can make up the black and yellow stick man using the same method as for Father Christmas. To make the stick man on p.13, weave a square scoubidou. Cut out circles from foam board, each 3.5cm (1³⁄₈in) in diameter, to make the hat.

Pen pals

You will need...
- 1 ball-point pen refill
- glue and scissors

To make the square scoubidou pen:
- 2 x 45cm (18in) pink threads
- 2 x 45cm (18in) blue threads

To make the round scoubidou pen:
- 1 red thread
- 1 pink thread
- 1 yellow thread
- 1 orange thread

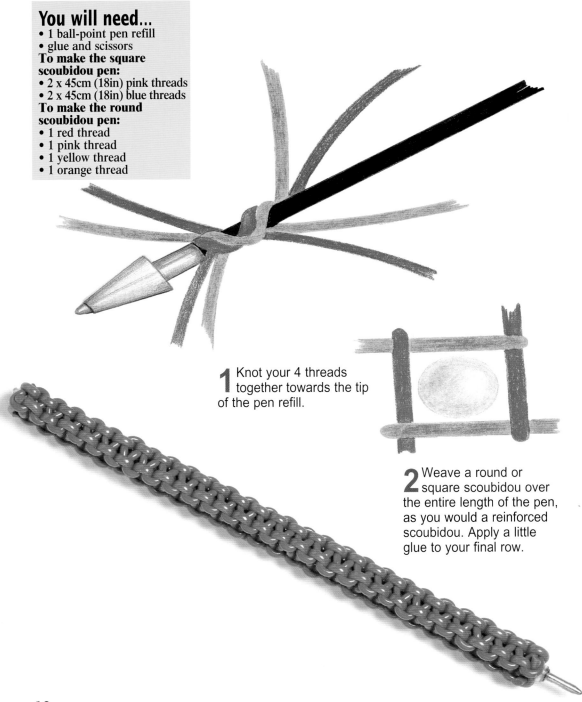

1 Knot your 4 threads together towards the tip of the pen refill.

2 Weave a round or square scoubidou over the entire length of the pen, as you would a reinforced scoubidou. Apply a little glue to your final row.

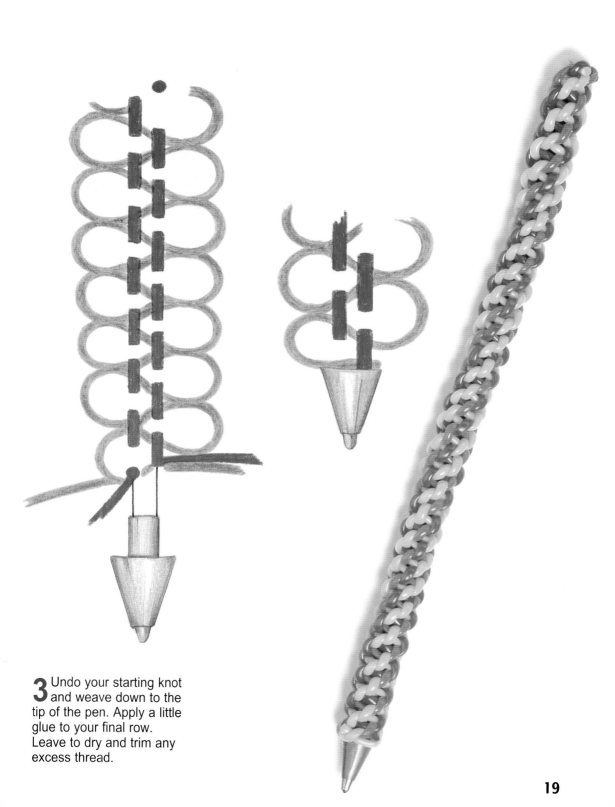

3 Undo your starting knot and weave down to the tip of the pen. Apply a little glue to your final row. Leave to dry and trim any excess thread.

Animal magic

You will need...

- black paint for use on plastic
- plastic egg
- 2 pink feathers
- corkscrew
- pink foam board
- black pompom 25mm (1in) in diameter
- 2 moving eyes 1cm (³/₈in) in diameter
- 6 x 90cm (36in) red threads
- wire

Dancing ostrich

1 Paint your egg. Leave to dry. Make 2 holes in the underside with a corkscrew to house the legs. Next, make up the legs. Take 2 x 45cm (18in) red threads and weave a round scoubidou 7.5cm (3in) long reinforced with a length of wire. Start from a hidden knot. Leave 2cm (³/₄in) excess wire at your starting point. Make up the second leg in the same way. Next, make the neck using 6 red threads. Weave a reinforced round 6-strand scoubidou for 5.5cm (2¹/₄in). Leave 2cm (³/₄in) excess wire at each end.

2 Using the template, cut out 4 feet from your pink foam board. Cut out the circle in the centre on the two top feet. Work your wire as indicated in the diagram and glue it between the 2 parts of the feet to help keep your ostrich upright. Leave to dry.

3 Insert the two feet into the 2 holes in the egg and glue. Glue the eyes onto your pompom. Glue the head onto the neck. Insert the neck into the hole and glue. Stick your feathers onto the body.

feet x 4

Animal magic

Puppy love

Starting from a hidden knot, weave a reinforced spiral scoubidou 3.5cm (1³⁄₈in) in length to make the body. Leave 5mm (³⁄₁₆in) excess wire at one end and 2cm (³⁄₄in) at the other. Weave a 2cm (³⁄₄in) white scoubidou to make the tail. Apply glue to your 2cm (³⁄₄in) wire and insert into the tail.

Take a 5cm (2in) length of wire. At one end, weave a square scoubidou over 1cm (³⁄₈in) with 2 x 10cm (4in) black threads and starting from a hidden knot. Trim the threads and glue. Thread a white bead onto the wire. Make a second scoubidou identical to the first. Thread on a white bead. Finish by making a third scoubidou. Trim and glue.

Add moving eyes and a pompom for the nose. Shape the head to make it round. Make the front legs from 2 x 6cm (2³⁄₈in) reinforced threads and the hind legs from 2 reinforced threads 8cm (3¹⁄₈in) length. Push the head onto the body and glue the legs onto each side.

Pinky pig

Apply a layer of glue to a cork and wind a pink thread around it, securing both ends with pins. Remove the pins when dry. Make up 4 reinforced round scoubidous 1.5cm (⁵⁄₈in) in length, leaving 1cm (³⁄₈in) excess wire at each end. Use a pin to make 4 holes in the body to accommodate the legs. Apply a little glue and insert them into the body. Leave to dry. Reinforce a 2.5cm (1in) thread using 3cm (1¹⁄₈in) wire. Wind it around the point of a pencil to curl it.

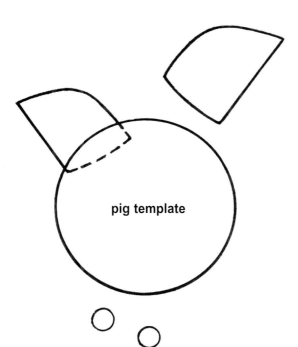

pig template

Glue a circle of pink foam board onto the back end of the cork. Insert the tail into this circle. Copy the templates and cut out a head, ears and nostrils. Make the snout from a reinforced round scoubidou 1.5cm (⁵⁄₈in) in length. Glue the ears onto the head and the head onto the body. Glue the snout and insert. Finally, glue on the nostrils and moving eyes.

Cool keyrings

You will need...
- scoubidou threads in various colours
- keyrings
- small pompoms
- moving eyes and bell
- beads

Ring your bell

Make up a reinforced round scoubidou 13cm (5in) in length using 2 green and white threads and one 15cm (6in) wire, leaving 1cm (3/8in) excess wire at each end. Bring the two ends of the scoubidou together to form a loop and twist the two ends of wire together. Glue on eyes and a pompom to make the nose. Secure the bell and the keyring to the wire.

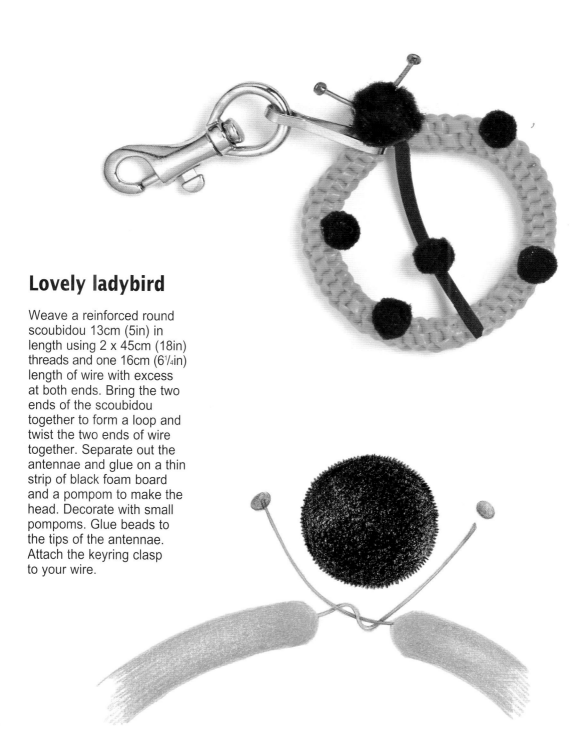

Lovely ladybird

Weave a reinforced round
scoubidou 13cm (5in) in
length using 2 x 45cm (18in)
threads and one 16cm (6¼in)
length of wire with excess
at both ends. Bring the two
ends of the scoubidou
together to form a loop and
twist the two ends of wire
together. Separate out the
antennae and glue on a thin
strip of black foam board
and a pompom to make the
head. Decorate with small
pompoms. Glue beads to
the tips of the antennae.
Attach the keyring clasp
to your wire.

Cool keyrings

Turkish hat

Nosey dog

Tie your scoubidou knot around the keyring. Weave a 6cm (2³/₈in) round scoubidou using 1 x 45cm (18in) yellow thread and 1 x 45cm (18in) orange thread. Finish off your scoubidou, trimming only the orange threads. Thread 1 yellow bead onto each yellow thread. Knot your thread around the bead. Glue down and trim, leaving 5mm (³/₁₆in) excess scoubidou. Roll up and glue half of your scoubidou back on itself, leaving beads on each side. Secure your work by tying a thread around it while it dries. Glue eyes onto the beads and glue on your pompom to make a nose.

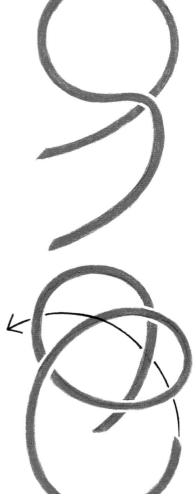

1 Take 1 x 90cm (36in) length of blue thread. Make a first loop and then a second over the top of the first.

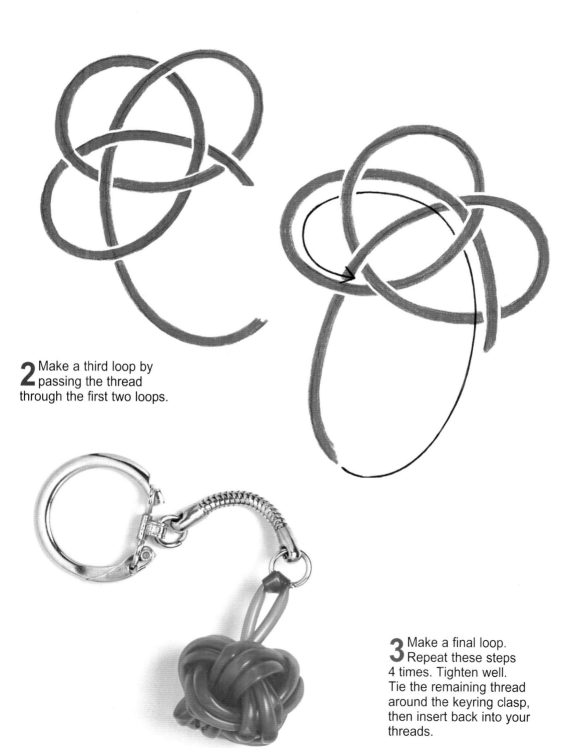

2 Make a third loop by passing the thread through the first two loops.

3 Make a final loop. Repeat these steps 4 times. Tighten well. Tie the remaining thread around the keyring clasp, then insert back into your threads.

Juicy jewellery

You will need...
- 6 red cabochons 7mm (¹/₄in) in diameter
- 1 spring clasp with bead tip
- 1 ring base
- 1 pair clip-on earrings
- 2 wires to reinforce your necklace (48cm/19in and 50cm/20in)
- 1 x 90cm (36in) yellow thread
- 1 x 90cm (36in) red thread
- 1 x 46cm (18in) hollow red thread
- 1 x 48cm (19in) hollow red thread
- glue
- scissors and wire-cutters

Cabochon supports
Weave your yellow and red threads in pairs. Knot the 3 threads with the fourth thread in the centre. Weave as you would a round row. Complete two rows and apply some glue. Trim any excess thread. Glue your cabochons onto your starting knot.

Ring
Make up a cabochon support and glue it onto a ring base.

Earrings
Make up 2 cabochon supports and glue them onto a pair of clip-on earrings.

Necklace
1 Insert your 48cm (19in) length of wire into a 46cm (18in) length of red thread and your 50cm (20in) length of wire into a 48cm (19in) length of red thread.

2 Make up one cabochon support. Before you tighten your second row, thread your reinforced red threads through, positioning the support at their centre. Position your 48cm (19in) reinforced red thread above the 50cm (20in) thread. Pull tight and glue. Leave to dry and trim your threads. Assemble another two cabochon supports in the same way, each approx. 4cm (1¹/₂in) from the central support on either side.

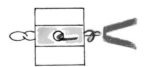

3 At each end of your necklace, wind one of your two ends of wire around the other. Insert your wire into the bead tip and wrap it around. Glue your bead tip and secure.

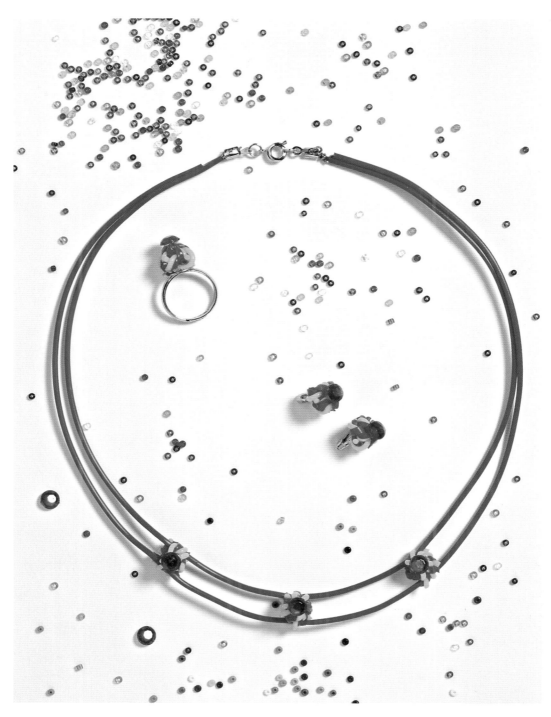

Accessorize now!

You will need...
- 1 clasp
- 3 x 45cm (18in) black threads
- 1 x 45cm (18in) red thread
- 1 x 20cm (8in) nylon thread
- glue and scissors

Red and black bracelet

Starting with a standard knot, weave a 17cm (6³/₄in) round scoubidou using 4 scoubidou threads and a 20cm (8in) length of nylon thread in the centre. Finish off by applying a little glue. Undo your starting knot and weave a row. Secure with a little glue. Leave to dry and trim your scoubidou threads. Attach the clasp to your nylon thread by tying three knots. Tighten and secure with glue.

Blue bracelet

You will need...
- 40cm (16in) nylon thread
- 1 clasp
- 39 silver beads
- 2 x 90cm (36in) blue threads
- glue and scissors

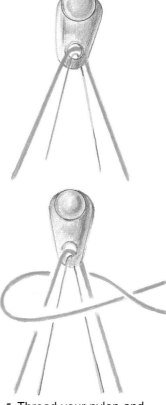

1 Thread your nylon and 1 blue thread into the clasp, placing your blue scoubidou thread on top of the nylon. Position the second blue thread as indicated in the diagram.

2 Start weaving. Make a loop and pass the thread through. Pull tight. Make a second loop in the opposite direction using the same thread as for the first loop. Make loops to the left and right to make a 1.5cm (⁵⁄₈in) braid.

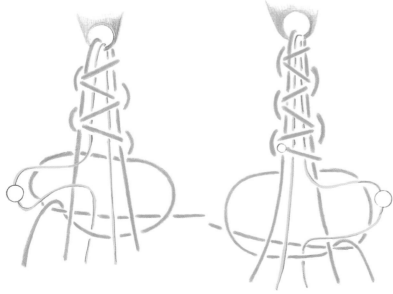

3 Now add your beads. Pull one of your nylon threads out to the side. Thread on a bead. Put your nylon thread back into the centre and tighten your work. Start braiding again. Pull your other nylon thread out to the other side and thread on another bead. Put the nylon thread back into the centre and tighten. Thread on a bead on each side of your work over 14cm (5¹⁄₂in). Finish with a 1.5cm (⁵⁄₈in) braided section with no beads. Glue and trim your blue threads. Attach the clasp to your nylon threads.

Accessorize now!

Panther brooch

Weave a reinforced round scoubidou for 16cm (6¼in) using 2 x 90cm (36in) lengths of pink thread. Leave 5mm (³/₁₆in) of your 17cm (6¾in) wire hanging out at each end. Glue your scoubidou and hold it in place with some sewing thread. Transfer the templates below onto foam board and cut them out. Glue them on and add moving eyes. Glue on a brooch between your panther's ears.

Green and black hair slide

Make up 6 green and black beads following the same method as for the cabochon supports on page 28. Weave two round scoubidou rows using 2 green threads and 2 black threads 15cm (6in) in length. Glue your beads onto a 7cm (2¾in) hair slide.

Eyes hair slide

1 Starting from a hidden knot, make up a square scoubidou using 2 orange threads and 2 yellow threads. Position your threads as shown in the diagram and begin.

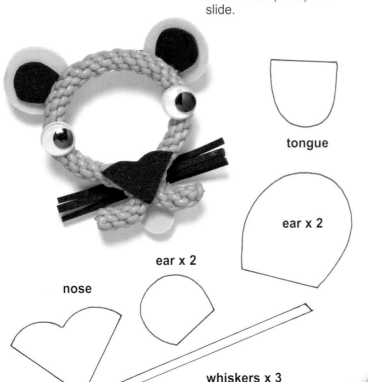

tongue

ear x 2

ear x 2

nose

whiskers x 3

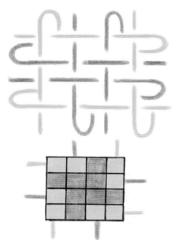

Pink hair slide

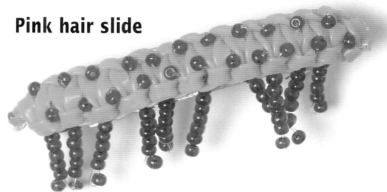

2 Using the diagram as a guide, pass your threads over and under. Tighten well. You should now have a square made up of 16 smaller squares.

This hair slide uses the same method as the blue bracelet on page 30. Use 1 x 45cm (18in) pink scoubidou thread, 1 x 10cm (4in) nylon thread and 1 x 30cm (12in) nylon thread to make rows of 7 beads. Thread on your first beads when you make your second knot. Finish your row. Make up each

row of beads by threading one bead onto the other nylon thread on the right at the same time. Alternate by threading on a single bead on the left. Repeat over 6cm (2³/₈in). Glue and trim. Glue your work onto a 5cm (2in) hair slide.

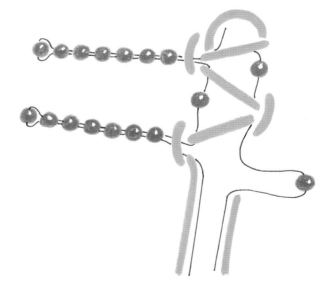

3 Continue to work in this way until you have a scoubidou 4.5cm (1³/₄in) long. Glue down your final row. Leave to dry and trim your threads. Glue on eyes and a pompom for a nose. Glue your scoubidou onto a 4cm (1¹/₂in) hair slide.

Pocahontas family

Sleepy baby

Weave a 1.5cm (⅝in) round scoubidou using 4 red threads. Glue on a pompom for the head. Transfer the template onto a leather chamois or piece of felt and cut out. Fold B and then C over A and glue. Fold in E, then glue D over C. Fold and glue F over G. Decorate with 6 beads.

Pocahontas

Weave a 3cm (1⅛in) round scoubidou in red to make the body. Make up the arms (6cm/2⅜in) and legs (7cm/2¾in) from 2 reinforced red threads and thread them into the body. Transfer one of the dress templates opposite onto a leather chamois or a piece of felt and cut it out. Decorate it with beads or acrylic paint. Put the dress onto the body and glue the edges together. Glue a 6cm (2⅜in) plait made from pipe-cleaners onto the pompom that will make up the head. Thread 3 beads onto some nylon and tie around each plait. Roll up a 7cm (2¾in) pipe-cleaner and glue it onto the back of the head. Glue the head to the body and leave to dry thoroughly.

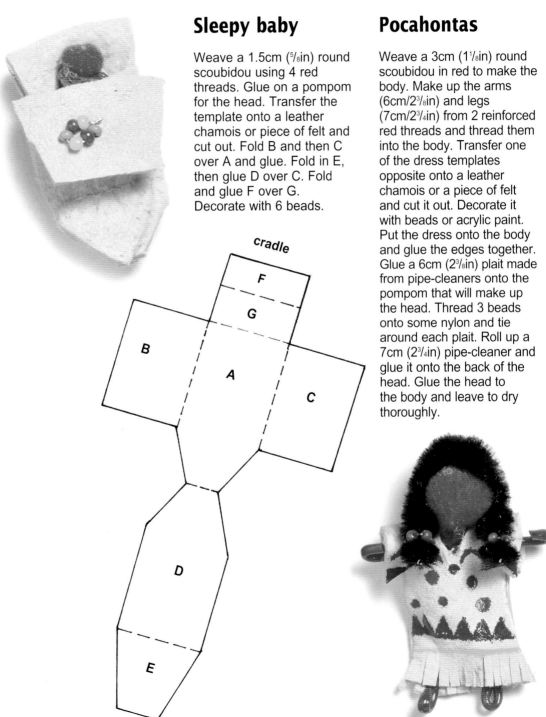

cradle

The brave

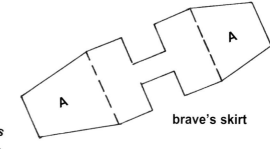

brave's skirt

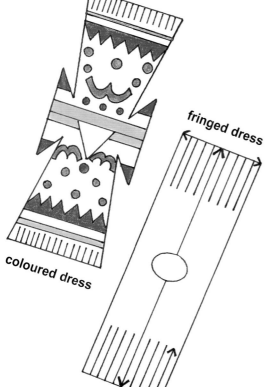

fringed dress

coloured dress

Weave a 3.5cm (1⅜in) round scoubidou in red to make the body. Make up the arms (6cm/2⅜in) and legs (8cm/3⅛in) using 2 reinforced red threads and thread them into your scoubidou as you go along. Glue a 3.5cm (1⅜in) length of pipe-cleaner onto your pompom to make the brave's plait. Thread 3 beads onto some nylon and tie around the plait. Transfer the template for the skirt onto a leather chamois or some felt and cut it out. Secure it onto your brave with some nylon. Fold up the two parts marked A and glue on beads to decorate.

 **Numbers and letters**

Attaching your magnets

Work with small magnets and glue on 2 for each letter or number. Attach your magnets to the largest areas of your letters and numbers, e.g. where 2 scoubidous cross.

Making your numbers and letters

Make your letters and numbers from 4-strand reinforced scoubidous, starting from a standard knot. Leave approx. 3mm (¹/₈in) excess wire in sections that need to be inserted into other scoubidous. Insert and glue different sections of the letters together to assemble them. In this book we have made all the letters using round scoubidous and all the numbers from square scoubidous.

**Letters and numbers
made from 1 scoubidou**
C, G, I, J, L, M, N, O, P, Q,
S, U, V, W, Z, 0, 1, 2, 3, 5,
6, 7, 9.

**Letters and numbers
made from 2 scoubidous**
A, D, K, R, T, Y, 8.

**Letters and numbers
made from 3 scoubidous**
B, E, F, H, X, 4.

Numbers and letters

Playground fun

You will need...

- 5 green scoubidou threads
- 5 pink scoubidou threads
- 1 x A4 (US letter) sheet of pink foam board
- 2 x 18.5cm (7¼in) wooden skewers
- 2 clear glass beads 9mm (³/₈in) in diameter
- small glass beads 5mm (³/₁₆in) in diameter in pink (x 4) and green (x 6)
- 6 x 30cm (12in) wire
- 2 x 14cm (5½in) wire (for the large supports on the slide)
- 2 x 10cm (4in) wire (middle supports)
- 2 x 6.5cm (2½in) wire (small supports)
- scissors and wire-cutters
- glue

Slide

1 Taking 1 x 90cm (36in) pink thread and 1 x 90cm (36in) green thread, weave 2 reinforced square scoubidous 11.5cm (4½in) in length around 14cm (5½in) wire to make the large supports for the slide. To make the middle supports, weave 2 reinforced round scoubidous 7cm (2¾in) in length with 60cm (24in) pink and green threads and 10cm (4in) wire. Make the small supports from 2 reinforced square scoubidous 4cm (1½in) in length made with pink and green threads 30cm (12in) in length. Leave 5mm (³/₁₆in) excess wire at the end of each support. Finish off your scoubidous.

2 Cut 1 green thread and 1 pink thread into 3 x 30cm (12in) lengths. Reinforce them with wire. Make 2 plaits with 3 x 30cm (12in) lengths of thread, one using 1 pink and 2 green threads and the other with 1 green and 2 pink threads. Twist them around and thread beads onto the ends.

3 Cut out a 3cm x 20cm (1¹/₈in x 8in) rectangle from foam board. Glue your plaits onto the sides and hold in place until dry. Attach the supports by threading your excess wire into the plaits. Secure with a little glue.

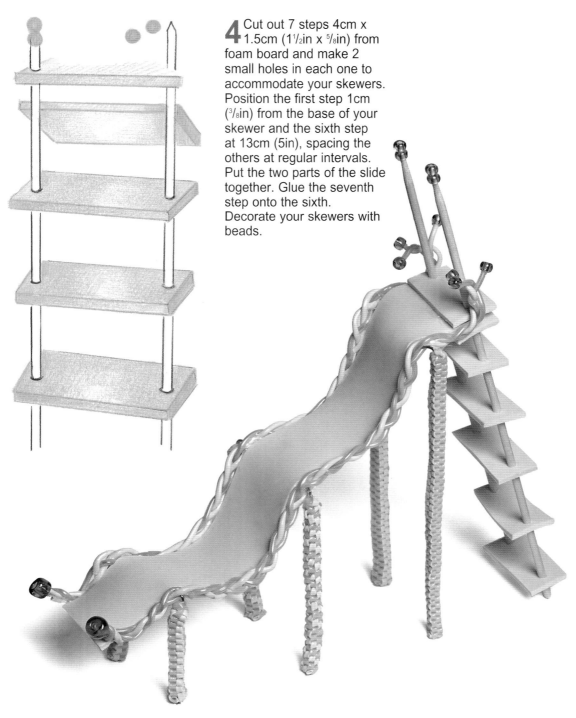

4 Cut out 7 steps 4cm x 1.5cm (1½in x ⅝in) from foam board and make 2 small holes in each one to accommodate your skewers. Position the first step 1cm (⅜in) from the base of your skewer and the sixth step at 13cm (5in), spacing the others at regular intervals. Put the two parts of the slide together. Glue the seventh step onto the sixth. Decorate your skewers with beads.

Playground fun

You will need...

- 10 x 90cm (36in) green scoubidou threads
- 1 x 12cm (4³/₄in) red scoubidou thread
- 1 x 12cm (4³/₄in) and 5 x 16cm (6¹/₄in) lengths of wire
- 5m (20ft) nylon thread
- small glass beads in yellow (x 150) and red (x 220)
- 1 ping-pong ball painted green
- 1 yellow pipe-cleaner
- 1 red pipe-cleaner
- 2 moving eyes 9mm (³/₈in) in diameter
- needle, glue, scissors and wire-cutters
- 14.5cm (5³/₄in) wooden skewer

Spider's web

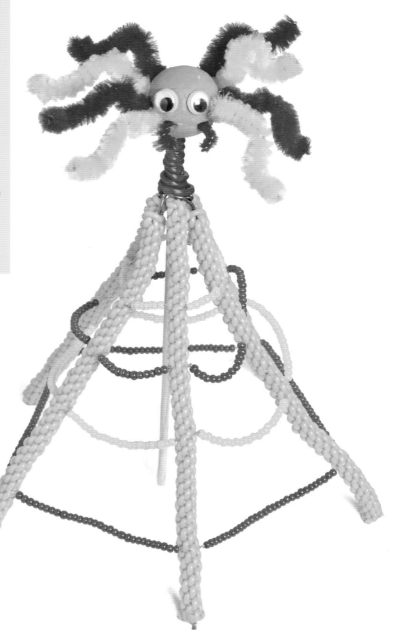

1 To make up each support leg, plait 2 x 90cm (36in) threads. Make 5 round scoubidous 13cm (5in) in length with a 16cm (6¼in) length of wire to reinforce. Start from a hidden knot and leave 1.5cm (⅝in) excess wire. Assemble the skewer with the point upwards. Position your 5 scoubidous around the skewer and attach them 2.5cm (1in) from the point using the excess wires. Reinforce your red thread with some wire. Wind it around the skewer for 2cm (¾in) to hide the wires. Leave the point of the skewer sticking out.

level 1
40cm (16in) nylon
start 3cm (1⅛in)
from the top
7 beads per row

level 2
90cm (36in) nylon
start 5cm (2in) from the top
14 beads per row

level 3
1.5m (60in) nylon
start 7.5cm (3in) from the top
23 beads per row

level 4
2m (80in) nylon
start 10.5cm (4⅛in) from the top
30 beads per row

2 Glue moving eyes onto your ball. Use a needle to make 2 holes and stick on 1cm (⅜in) jaws. Cut 4 yellow legs and 4 red legs 4.5cm (1¾in) in length. Make holes either side of the eyes and stick them into the ball. Push the head onto the skewer and glue down.

3 Make up strings of beads to sit between the upright legs. Knot a nylon thread at its centre. Tie it around the first leg with two knots and a little glue. Thread beads onto the double thread. Tie 2 knots and wind the thread around the second leg. Knot twice and continue. Arrange your rows as indicated in the diagram.

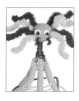

Playground fun

You will need...
- 2 x 5cm (2in) lengths of nylon
- 3 x 90cm (36in) blue threads
- 1 piece yellow thread
- glue, scissors, wire-cutters

To make the legs:
- 4 x 15.5cm (6⅛in) wooden skewers
- 8 x 45cm (18in) yellow threads
- 8 x 45cm (18in) orange threads

To make the crossbar:
- 1 x 18.5cm (7¼in) wooden skewer
- 2 x 90cm (36in) yellow threads
- 2 x 90cm (36in) orange threads

To make the trapeze:
- 1 x 4.5cm (1¾in) piece of skewer
- 2 x 5cm (2in) wires
- 2 x 6cm (2⅜in) blue threads

To make the swing:
- 1 x 45cm (18in) blue thread
- 2 x 30cm (12in) yellow threads
- 2 x 6cm (2⅜in) hollow blue threads
- 2 x 7cm (2¾in) wires

To make the knotted rope:
- 1 x 24cm (9½in) hollow blue scoubidou thread

Climbing frame

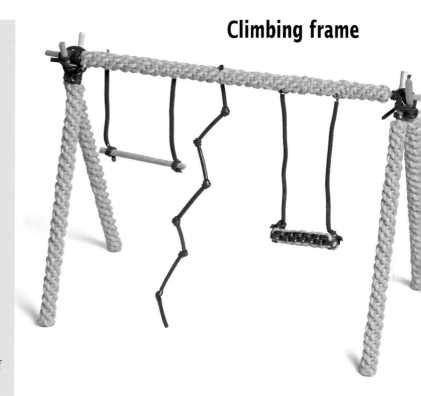

Frame
Weave one round scoubidou around each skewer using 2 threads in each colour, starting from a standard 4-strand knot. Start 1.5cm (⅝in) from the base of your skewer and plait an 11.5cm (4½in) long scoubidou around the skewer. Apply a little glue to your final row. Undo your starting knot and weave towards the end if necessary. Make up the crossbar of the frame in the same way, leaving 2cm (¾in) at the start and plaiting a 14.5cm (5¾in) scoubidou.

Trapeze
Knot your 2 blue threads around the skewer and glue down. Reinforce the threads with wire. Finally, push them into the crossbar of the frame and glue down.

Knotted rope
Tie 6 knots in your scoubidou thread. Glue your rope to the top of your frame.

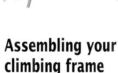

See-saw

Taking 2 x 45cm (18in) red threads, weave a reinforced square scoubidou 5.5cm (2¹/₈in) in length around a 3cm (1¹/₈in) length of wire. Starting from a hidden knot, weave a reinforced square scoubidou using 2 x 10cm (4in) red threads. Leave 5mm (³/₁₆in) excess wire. Push your small scoubidou into the centre of the larger one and bring the wire out at the other side. Thread on a bead and bend the wire over. Weave two 6-strand rectangular scoubidous 1.5cm (⁵/₈in) in length using 20cm (8in) long white threads and 10cm (4in) red threads. Glue them to each side of the see-saw.

Swing

Make a 6-strand rectangular scoubidou 3cm (1¹/₈in) in length. Reinforce your two blue threads, leaving 5mm (³/₁₆in) excess wire at each end. The easiest way to make your swing is to insert your reinforced threads into either side of the seat and glue them down. Thread the other ends between two rows in your crossbar scoubidou and glue.

Assembling your climbing frame

Push the legs into the corners of a 16cm x 9cm (6¹/₄in x 3¹/₂in) piece of card. Tie them in pairs with your nylon thread. Bend any ends back. Assemble your crossbar scoubidou between the upright supports. Secure by tying a blue thread around several times and adding a little glue. Leave to dry.

Benches

Weave 4 reinforced round scoubidous 1cm (³/₈in) in length to make the bench legs. Leave 1cm (³/₈in) excess wire. Weave an 8-strand rectangular scoubidou over 4.5cm (1³/₄in). Push the legs into this scoubidou and glue down.

45